Evolution
of the
Heart, Mind, Body, and Soul

by
Corey T. Tate

Credits:

Cover Design and Interior Art: Barbara Ann Swanson

Text Design: Dan Maio

Composition and Production: Graphics West, Inc., Colorado Springs, Colorado

Printing: C & M Press, Denver Colorado

Copyright © 2001 by Corey T. Tate

All rights reserved. Printed in the United States of America. No part of this book may be used or reproduced by any mechanical, photographic, or electronic process, or in the form of a phonographic recording, without permission of the publisher.

ISBN: 0-9721172-0-2

Published by
It Is Written Publications
P.O. Box 75984
Colorado Springs, CO 80970-5984
e-mail: itiswrittenpub@aol.com

Dedication

To my parents:

My daddy, Otis Tate, I miss you dearly. May you rest in peace.

My mama, Ruby M. Tate, I finally did it! I became somebody.

The poem "I Am" is dedicated to my parents.

Contents

Part I: The Heart

A Hold on Me	2
A Pledge of One	4
A Wish	5
Alone	6
A Good Day	7
An Angel	9
Can I Get to Know You?	10
Eternally	12
Expressions	13
From the Heart	14
Good Morning	15
Heaven Sent	16
Let Me	17
Let's Get Together	18
Lost Love	19
Merry Christmas	20
Missing You	22
Mother Hen	23
My Heart	24
My Pawncheeta	25
My Valentine (Romantic)	26
Patience	27
Reinforcement	28
Someone Special	29
Soul Mate	30
Tell Me	32
Ten and Ten	33
The Blues	35
The Chosen One	36
The Cycle of Love	38

The One	39
The Right One	41
The World Is Mine	42
Thinking of You	43
Unconditional Love	44
Wake Up!	45
Welcome Home	46
What Is Love?	47
When My Eyes Cry	48
Will You?	49
You	51
Your Wedding Day	52

Part II: The Mind

A Good Night's Sleep	54
A Small-Town Girl	55
A Vision	57
Discouraged	59
Dysfunctional Family	60
Hail the Queen	62
Help Me Cope	63
I'm a Man!	64
Inspiration	65
Is It You?	66
Just a Guy	67
Pieces of a Dream	69
Resignation	70
Responsible	72
Roll Call!	73
Snap!	75
The Big "F" Over	77
The Finish Line	78
The Passage	79
When He Thinks	81
When Will the Madness Stop?	82

Part III: The Body

Animal Instinct	86
As We Lay	87
Caress Me	89
Fiend	90
Fire and Desire	91
Have You Ever?	92
In the Rain	93
Is It Me You're Looking For?	94
Let's Get It On!	95
Seduction	96
Zoomin'!	97

Part IV: The Soul

A Message	100
A Prayer	103
A Stormy Season	104
A True Friend	106
A Queen	107
Get Right!	108
Happy Birthday!	109
I Am!	110
Knowledge, Purpose, Peace	111
Lock and Key	112
Midday Prayer	113
Mother to Child	114
My Valentine (Spiritual)	116
Oh, How Sweet It Is!	118
On Bended Knee	119
Our Days Are Numbered	121
Second Time Around (Born Again)	122
Strong Men Keep Coming On!	124
The End Is Near	126
Your Journey Continues	128

Acknowledgments

First and foremost, I want to thank my Lord and Savior, Jesus Christ. Without Him, I would not be. Without Him, these words would not have been expressed.

Second, I want to thank all the people I've ever encountered throughout my life's journey, whether they had a positive or negative, happy or sad, loving or caring, hurtful or painful impact upon me. You all enabled me, molded me into the man I am today.

Last but not least, a special thanks to my *true* friends who had my back during the stormy seasons and the sunshine and rainbow-filled days. To the Bardwell family, Otis Dancy, Jason and Heather McCarty, Valerie Gresham, Elmore Williams, Ephriam Fitzgerald, Evva "Mama Cook" Cook, and Michelle Nelson. Thank you all for your love and support over the years. Real and true friends are truly hard to come by in this day and age. May God Keep you all in His grace until the end of time. I love you all. God bless!

Corey T. Tate

Part I
The Heart

A Hold on Me

My love for you is true.
From time to time I don't know what to do.

Sometimes I need you close to me.
Can you feel my heart beat?
Can you feel my hair and fingernails grow?

Sometimes I can do without you near me.
Not close, but at a distance.

I feel like a fiend.
Like a crackhead wondering when, where, and how
I'll get my next fix.
Oh Lord! Put me in the mix!

What am I to do?
I know that I love and care about you.

Sometimes I wonder am I really in love with you?
What am I to do?
You have this hold on me.
Damn! What am I to do?

Is this real?
Is it true?
What am I to do?

Sometimes I feel like I understand, as if I'm in control.
But damn! On the other hand, I feel like I'm losing control.
It feels like my heart and mind are playing tricks on me.

What am I to do?
God, my Father up above, deliver me from this madness.
Deliver me from these issues that I keep.
What are they?
Why are they in my heart and my mind?
Give me peace!

Stop!

I am the master of my faith.
I am the captain of my soul.
Remove this hold that's upon me that I know.

Am I in love?
Is it love?
Remove this hold on me!

A Pledge of One

What kind of man would I be if I didn't tell you the little things
that let you know how much I care about you and love you?

For example, opening the door for you.
Helping you with your chair and your coat.
Or wiping the crumbs from your face after you eat.

When it comes to me loving you, my love is like the bottomless pit of a
well that's endless.
It's deep.

It's mental, too.
Like me telling you how beautiful you are.
That your dress looks good on you.
That your lipstick brings out the fullness of your lips.
By the way, give Daddy a kiss.

These are endless verbal expressions
of me letting you know how much I love you.

It's physical, too.
For example, when you tell me what you want and what you need.
Whether it's licking you up and down,
going downtown, or all around town.
Your wish is truly my command.
My mission is to please you.
However or whatever you want me to do, I'll do it because I love you.

This is our world.
Two people coming together,
going into wars and battles against the world as one.
Together forever we'll rule the world
as you and I,
as we,
as one.

I thank God for you.

I love you.

A Wish

When you're feeling down and out, blue.

Look outside into God's heavenly skies.

Find that flickering star—the North Star.

Close your eyes and make a wish.

Wish that I were there with you—
hugging you, kissing you, loving you,
supporting and appreciating you.

Every queen needs a king in her life.

From near or from afar, if you wish upon the North Star,
I'll always be with you no matter where you are.

Close your eyes and feel our spirits connect as one.

Can you feel me deep inside your soul?

My love will always live and dwell within your heart.

My Queen, your wish is my command.

Make a wish.

Forget me not.

Alone

It would be nice to share time with someone special.

To hold hands while walking in the park;
to share malts and kisses; to be lovey-dovey
and say how much we care for one another.

It would be so nice to be in love;
to share joy and laughter, pain and sorrow;
to tell one another that we'll always
be there for each other.

When a man loves a woman
and the chemistry is truly there,
along with trust and honesty,
beware!

When all of these characteristics
are brought together between two people like a brew of stew,
it's time to drop to one knee and ask that woman to marry you!

Then walk down that aisle with your heart pumping fast;
your nerves giving you the jitters
as the minister recites the words of matrimony.

Oh, God!

I'm no longer alone,
but married as one at last!

A Good Day

As I rise, I rub my eyes.
I place my hands in front of my face.
I pray to God that it's you.
But it's only a pillow or two.

Why can't it be you by my side?
You!

The last time I saw your face,
I saw the world in a different light,
like a blind man who was blessed with sight.
Your smile brings me warmth,
full of joy and happiness.

Every time I see you, I have a vision of children, our children.
A blessing of offspring is greater than me, man.

How can a woman touch a man's heart?
His heart can first be touched in adolescence.
If a woman can bring out the child in a man,
she will not only win his heart, but his soul.

As the day passes on, all my thoughts are of you.
Where can you be?
Where are you?
Hopefully you are safe, happy, and at peace,
wherever you are.

As the day comes to an end,
I kneel down again on bended knees,
praying to God my soul to keep.
I thank Him for helping me through yet another day
of you being away from me.
He has helped me through 364 days thus far.
But tomorrow will be the day that He'll bring you back my way.

I pray for a good night's sleep
so I can open my eyes tomorrow morning
and see a sunshine-filled day.
When I lay my eyes upon your pretty brown eyes,
your glorious smile, your caramel skin—
that day will truly be a good day.

I love you.

An Angel

An angel can be a lighter shade of brown.

May you continue to strive beyond the highest of heights.
Your aim is for heaven, God's land.
If you fall short, at least you'll be amongst the moon and stars.

Life is merely a dream of joy and pain.

You're a Nubian Queen.
You'll always be amongst the moon and stars.
As you hold the stars in your hand, remember me—
a friend who's afar, thinking of you.

An angel of a lighter shade of brown, a Nubian Queen,
a woman who can do anything.

May God bless you with peace, love, and harmony.

My friend, I love you.

My Nubian Queen, an angel, my angel,
who has my heart in her hands.
Forget me not, as you soar away, flying through God's heavenly skies.

My angel, may you have peace!

Forget me not!

Can I Get to Know You?

From time to time, in my quiet moments,
I sit and wonder while thinking of you.
I wonder how you're doing.
I wonder how you're feeling.
I wonder if you're safe.
I wonder if you're at peace.
I wonder if you're thinking of me too.

When I think of you, I envision the peace of a cool summer breeze.
As when the branches upon trees
effortlessly rock their leaves with ease.

Peace is thinking of you.

When I think of you, I envision a dozen angels flying through the air,
empowering God's grace.
When I think of you, I envision God's hands upon you.

When I see you, my first thought is not to hug or kiss you;
I want to sit you down and greet you
by washing and massaging your feet.

Your determination,
your desire,
your strength,
your inner and external beauty move me.

Your facial features display your culture and your heritage.
Your asset curves were truly made by God's grace.
Your eyes are so lovely that
I want to look deep inside of them to make a connection
with your soul.

When your hair is straight, I want to let my fingers do the walking.
When your hair is curly, I want to pull and twist it
so that it can bounce back into place.
When your hair is up, I want to gently kiss your neck.

I want to find out if we're compatible.
I want to get deep with.
I want to get intellectual with you.
But first, most of all, I want to get to know you.
Hello, my name is …
Can we be friends?

Eternally

It happened again.

God has blessed us, let us be in one another's presence again.

Like two old friends, we joked,
we laughed, and we shed a tear;
we even shared a kiss or two.

We reminisced about the good-old-days—
you liking me and me not giving you the time of day.

Life has truly brought us full circle.

360 degrees in a sphere of friendship
that will last until eternity passes.
In essence, our dying days.

No matter where we go, who we're with, we'll always be connected—
mentally, physically, and spiritually—
as friends until the end.

You're a true, dear friend.

Forget me not!

Expressions

Excuse me, may I have a moment of your time?
It'll be all right.
Just allow me to look deep into your eyes
and run my fingers through your hair.
It's so silky with sheen.
It smells like a cool summer breeze.
Is it ultra-sheen?

I love the way you walk.
I love your body's curves.
I love how you make your tongue roll
when you whisper sweet nothings to me as we snuggle and cuddle.
Oh, girl!

You're bad as you wanna be.
That's why you're my girl.
You go girl!

Making love to you means more to me than
the moon, the stars, and the mountains.
You mean everything to me.
You're my world.
You're the reason why I live.
You're the reason why I do what I do to support, please, satisfy,
and love you.

It's all for you, me, and we—our family.
You're my heart.

Remember this: *Expression!*

I love you.

From the Heart

When I look into your eyes, I can see the hurt and pain you've endured.

Who did this to you?

Oh, it's a shame.

What can I do to take away your hurt and pain?

What can I do to keep you from walking around
with a frown on your face
because you're angry, depressed, and full of hate?

Do you really want to kill his ass?

What will that solve?
It will only take away your freedom, your self-respect, your dignity.

No, not that.

Let me be a friend to you.

We can talk, share experiences and stories,
and cry and laugh together.

Life is full of both joy and pain, victory and defeat.

The key is to keep on moving and not miss a beat.

Remain steadfast and true to yourself and God, the Father up above.

Faith is the key to help you remove and conquer any and all problems
that will soon be known as *what was*.

Keep on!

Keeping on!

Good Morning

When the sun rises, you open your eyes.

As the sunlight shines upon your face, your eyes illuminate and glow, full of life, joy, and grace.

How beautiful they truly are, your pretty brown eyes.

Your eyes put the cool in a cool summer breeze.

Your eyes bring me peace when I'm dismayed.

Your glare melts me like butter on hot toast, oatmeal, and grits.

What I'm trying to say, is that I admire your pretty brown eyes.

What I'm trying to say most of all,
is that I admire the keeper of those pretty brown eyes.

What I'm really trying to say most of all is, "Good morning brown-eyes."

I hope you have a good day today.

Heaven Sent

Each night and day, I pray to God that He will bring you my way.
Only God knows how much I want you close to me.
Only God knows how much I want you with me.

I want a woman who will satisfy my every need.
I want a woman who can stimulate my mind, body, and soul.
I want a woman who fears God.
I want a woman who has direction.
I want a woman who's lovable, sweet, and true.

My dear,
my darling,
I want you because you complete me.

Put your hand inside of mine.
Interlock your fingers with mine.
We're joined together as one.
Baby, you're the one.

I will love you.
I will support you.
I will worship you
with all of my heart, mind, body, soul, and strength.

You're the chosen one.

Let Me

Hearing your voice brings peace
to my heart, my mind, my body, and my soul.

The warmth and sweetness of your voice remove the stress
running up and down my spine, shoulders, and neck.

I can feel the sweet joy of your beautiful smile.

I can feel the softness of your lips
when you kiss me good morning, goodbye, or hello.

The simplest thought of you sends chills up and down my spine.

I can't wait to see you and look deep inside your seductive brown eyes.

Let me remove all of your hurt and pain.

Let me be the one to serve you, I'll show you no shame.

Let me be your beacon, the light shining bright in your life.

Let me caress you when you need to be touched.

Let me hug you when you need love, warmth, and protection.

Let me wipe away your tears when you cry because you hurt so badly.

Let me be the one you call yours.

Let me be your man.

Let's Get Together

Roses are red and violets are blue,
your pretty white smile fills me up with joy too.
Your eyes are so beautiful
when their constant stare is fixed upon me.
Your body would make any dress or pair of jeans scream,
"Lord have mercy!"
Your personality is warm and gentle,
full of love and happiness, though touched by the experience of pain.
Your touch is so gentle and innocent,
like the softness of a newborn child.
Your heart is made of gold,
pumping the blood of honesty, joy, and passion.

You are you and I'm me.
We're both of royalty—Nubians.

May our friendship last until the end of time.
May our love pump through our veins
fueled by God, the Father, from up above.

Let's stay together.
No more meetin', greetin', and freakin'.
No more bumpin' and grindin' and lyin' as the players do.
Let's have something that's real—
a friendship, a companionship, a relationship, a marriage,
a family, and stability, too.

As God lays me down to sleep, I pray that my soul He'll keep.
I pray that before I die, He blesses me with all of these beautiful things,
because you are beautiful to me.

I love you!

From the heart.

Lost Love

Ever since you went away from me,
my mental and my physical went astray.

I wish you would've stayed, because I'm still in love with you girl.

Every night and day, I wish you never went away from me.

I wish you were near me, like you used to be.
Before all of this madness,
everything that I looked at would remind me of your smiling face.

Lately, my visions of you have been full of pain, tears, and sadness,
instead of joy, smiles, and happiness.

I've been a fool!

I was out and about meetin', greetin', and creepin'.

I was trying to be a player who crushed a lot.

I was looking for love in all the wrong places.

But love was at home with you.
That's where I should've been, too.

Now I'm crying the blues
because my nights in bed are cold and lonely without you.

What am I supposed to do now that you're gone?

My heart, my loved one is truly gone.

Love is a game that you must play to survive, not to win.

If you're trying to win, you'll be at home all alone in the cold
wishing that you could do things all over again.

Stop messing around!

Merry Christmas

I watch the snowflakes fall through the windowpane.
The fireplace is ablaze, chestnuts are roasting on an open fire,
and a pine-scent is floating through the air.

Our winter getaway, a cabin in the mountains,
is so peaceful, romantic, and seductive
that only a Hallmark card would dare to compare.

Dinner is prepared, the wine is chilled,
the presents are underneath the tree,
and the Persian rug is plush and fluffy awaiting our bodies.

As the sun sets high in the mountains, a beautiful,
bright reddish-orange glow beams off of your beautiful caramel face
as you get out of the car and close the door.

You enter the cabin with your arms full of gifts, candy,
and fruit baskets galore.

When you lay your eyes upon me,
you drop everything and run and jump
into my waiting, protective, love-filled arms.

You greet me with a big hug and a fat, juicy, love-filled kiss.
And the sweetest hello and I love you that you've ever expressed.

I thank God on this day for His birth and for enabling me to be here
with you.

Blessings of this kind are truly few and far between.

As I reminisce about the good and bad,
the happy and sad, the trying and blessed times of this past year,
I thank you.

As I kneel down on bended knees, my utmost thanks are
for you being in my life,
for you being by my side day and night.

Every day is Christmas to me
because I've been blessed with being with you.

I not only pray for another year with you,
I pray to God that I can spend my whole life with you.

This is my present to you.

I love you!

Merry Christmas!

Missing You

Every time I hear a sound, I turn around and pray to God it's you.
Every night and day, I wonder what I'll do the next time I see you.
Will I hug you?
Will I kiss you?
What will I do?
I'm just missing you.

Even though you're gone and many miles away,
I can still feel your soul and your spirit inside my mind and body
each and every day.
Is that weird?
Do you feel the same way?
I hope you do.
It's just a sign of me missing you.

I'm just a man trying to live and survive each and every day
as if it were my last.
But no matter what I do, I'm still missing you.

Life, especially love, is truly a game.
We're all trying to survive
because winning seems like it'll never be in reach to grasp.
All that we can do is hold onto the memories of the past,
the good and the bad, the happy and the sad.
We must live and learn from the past and pray for a future that'll last.

My body is calling for a little love and passion.
Everybody needs a little stimulation to keep them alive and satisfied.
I pray that someday soon God will bring you back to me,
back to the gentle clutch of my love-filled and protective arms.

Until then I'll continue to watch the sun rise and set.
At night I'll look into God's heavenly skies
and wish upon that flickering star;
wish that someday soon I'll stop missing you
and you'll no longer be afar.
You'll be standing in front of me;
we'll be looking deep into each other's eyes,
telling one another how much we love each other.

Until then I'll be thinking of you, because I'm missing you.

Mother Hen

When a mother hen flies from the coop,
she seeks food and shelter for her young.
The mother hen is the main caretaker, provider for her family.
She wears many hats:
a mother, a father, a teacher, a provider, and a protector.

A mother hen's job would be a lot easier
if the rooster were a real man who would take care of his responsibilities—
his lady hen and his baby chicks; not someone else's chicks.

A mother hen not only carries the burdens of her own problems,
but also those of her baby chicks.

Oh, mother hen, I wish you would let me be there for you.
Oh, mother hen, please remember you have a true friend in a rooster
that cares for and worries about you.
Oh, mother hen, I love you dearly.

Mother hen, fly from your coop.
Do what you gotta do.

This rooster will keep the memory of your beautiful smile alive.

The softness and warmth of your skin chill me.
Your determination and desire move me.

Oh, mother hen, even though you must fly away, I'll forget you not.

My Heart

During the cycle of life, decisions and mistakes are made,
life is given and taken from us on a daily basis.

We, as individuals, must be able to cope
with the cards that have been dealt to us by God.

It matters not how near or far I am from you,
my heart will always be with and yearn for you.

In time, all wounds from a broken heart will mend.
True love that's destined to be will come to pass,
regardless of the evil and error that dwell and lurk about
during the day and night.

Whether we're walking hand in hand along the waterfront
laughing, giggling, and sharing our thoughts with one another
under the glint of the stars and moonlight;
whether we're in different cities, states, countries, or just afar;
you'll always be in my heart.

My Pawncheeta

My Pawncheeta, whose smile is so bright
that I must put on my sunglasses to turn down the glaring light:

Your skin is so smooth, silky with sheen, like my caramel-colored satin sheets.

Your demeanor is so confident, filled with ambition, focus, and strength.

Your heart is made of gold that fuels every vein in your body
with the sweetest blood known to man from head to toe.

My Pawncheeta, who stands steadfast and true,
whose love is the sweetest thing that I've ever known:

Oh, how I love you.

Your laughter brings me joy.

Your voice puts me at ease and frees my mind of stress,
as if it were a cool summer breeze.
Your gentle touch makes my body shiver and quiver.

My Pawncheeta, you're my heart, my soul, and the reason why I live.
You're my everything.
You're my world.

My Pawncheeta, please be my wife.

My Pawncheeta, you complete me!

My Valentine (Romantic)

As I write to you this night, the room is dim,
filled with shadows from the flames of candles.
The room's atmosphere is filled with the seductive smell of incense
moving through the air.
The mood is truly right.

The soft and silky feel of my satin sheets reminds me
of your beautiful caramel skin.

My mind is reminiscing about when we were together last.
The fun, the laughter, and your pretty white smile
that always brightens up my day when I'm dismayed.

You bring me joy when I'm with you;
I feel so complete, at ease, at peace.
We truly have a total package, you and I.
It's my purpose and my mission, especially when I'm away from you,
to let you know how much I love and care about you.

Baby, I miss you.

Remember that every day is a special day for me
because you are my lady,
my heart, and my soul.
You're my life.
The reason why I chose you as mine?
Because you complete me.
You're the one.
I love you.

Sincerely,
Your Valentine

Patience

Patience is the ability to wait and not be tired by waiting.

Patience is the ability to understand
that others come before you do—priorities.

Patience is the ability to remain calm, understanding, steadfast, and true.

Patience is the ability to know that someday soon
we'll share secrets, joy, laughter, love, and pain.

Patience is the reality that I'm waiting on you to do what you have to do,
to take care of your responsibilities.

My patience wants you to know that I'm waiting for you
to share a moment of your time with me.

Patience displayed by a man who wants to touch
your mind, your body, and your soul.

Patience is the ability to wait for a good thing.

Patience, my dear, is waiting for you.

Reinforcement

As the sun sets, I'm sitting on my deck sipping on some cognac,
puffing on a stogy.

The cool summer breeze has definitely helped put my mind at ease.
But, all in all, I'm still thinking of you.

As night falls upon me, my buzz has definitely reached its zenith.
As I look up at the starlight that shines so bright,
it reminds me of all of those nights that we made love
under the flickering shadows of candlelight.
Your facial beauty was illuminated by the slow glow from the candles.

As I sit here reminiscing about our love,
a tear rolls down my face because I'm not near you.
I need to be with you because I love and miss you.

I pray to God that you're being trustworthy while you're away from me.

When a man loves a woman
it's okay for him to feel a little insecure when she's away from him.
It's just a sign that I truly love and miss you girl!
You're my world.

It's a shame that when two people are in love with one another
that they must be away from each other.
But the reunions are always memorable.

So, whether your lover is near or far,
reinforce that she's wanted, needed, and appreciated.
But most of all, loved.

Someone Special

As the world turns,
every second, every minute, every hour of the day that comes and goes
is known as the days of our lives.

In life, we may be blessed with the opportunity to meet,
to know someone special who will challenge us
to be the best that we can.
Whether it's mental or physical, they challenge us.

Our lives paths were paved before day one.
God, the Father, knew what type of man or woman we would become.
He projected our whole life cycle through the pupils of His eyes
before we were even conceived inside of the womb, the birthstone of life.

Because of our friendship, our trust and honesty,
our love, support, and compassion,
I've grown into the man that I've become.
You bring out the best in me.
This is the reason why I love you so.
This is the reason why I live.

Because of God, I am.
Because of God, I met you.
I thank Him for bringing you into my life.
I thank Him for you.
Thank you for being you.
I appreciate you.
I love you.
You're special to me.
You're someone special.

Soul Mate

As I sit in this room thinking of you,
I catch my mind wandering for a minute or two.
I sit here reflecting about where I am today,
reminiscing about the past and awaiting tomorrow—
the unknown, the future, a mystery.
Will it last?

I thank God for all of my accomplishments.
I thank Him for being the head of my life.
Without Christ, I don't know where I would be.
Father, God, I thank thee.

I've overcome the odds.
I put any and all critics to shame.
My journey has been long and hard, with many miles to go.
My walk has been both short and long in length.
But stride for stride, He's with me.
He never misses a beat.

No one really knows how heavy the burdens are that I keep.
I'm a man who stands alone.
One day I'll no longer stand alone,
but be united as one with my soul mate.
Until then I'll continue my journey upon the path
that my Father has placed before me.
When and where I'll meet my soul mate—
only God the Father knows the answer to that dream.
One day, this will no longer be a dream, but reality.

With God as my witness,
I'll have only one condition when it comes to my soul mate:
to love her unconditionally with all of my heart, mind, body, soul, and
strength.

I pledge my life to thee.
I'll go to any length to prove my love to the one Heaven sent
to be with me.
I'll die for you if that's what you want me to do.

United we stand and divided we fall,
my soul mate and I will be tighter than the core of a tree, solid as a rock,
too strong to fall.

Hand in hand, stride for stride we'll go.
We'll always tell one another how much we love, appreciate, and
cherish each other.
Our actions will speak loudly, supporting our words when we're
together.

Besides lovers, we'll be best friends.
We'll be able to talk about anything under the sun:
love, happiness, music, sadness, politics, the arts, biblical texts,
current events, stocks and bonds.
We'll have a commitment, a relationship, joined and united by God.

One day I'll no longer dream about your eyes,
beautiful as God's heavenly skies.
Your body, your spirit, your persona will be here with me.
Until that day, I'll always think of thee.
A Goddess, my Goddess, heaven-sent you'll be.
Have no fear, because when we least expect it,
God the Father will bring us together and unite us forever.
Thank you, Jesus!

Is that someone you?

Tell Me

As I sit here in the flickering candlelight, sipping on a little wine,
eased back in my easy chair,
my mind is wandering, but I'm thinking of you.

Oh, how I wish that your mind, body, and soul were here with me.
I wish that I were caressing you from head to toe.

Your skin is so soft.
Your hair is so fluffy, silky with sheen.
Your body smells so sweet and elegant, a scent only a rose could bring.
Your smile is so heartwarming, full of life, joy, and gleam.

Oh, how I wish I could be with you on this day.
I enjoy your company and presence.
In essence, your demeanor is strong-willed, with determination, desire,
and focus.
True strength is your character.

Oh, how I wonder how you actually feel about me.
Are you interested?
Do you care about me?
Do you want to get to know me?

Only you can answer these questions.
Only you can tell me where your heart and head are.

So, baby, what's it gonna be?

Tell me what you want.
Tell me what you need.
Tell me what's it gonna be.
Tell me your plea!
Tell me!

Ten and Ten

We knew each other for years.
We were little shorties with puppy love that grew into lust and love.
Finally, it came to pass.
We stayed together for ten days and ten nights.
It was so right.
Hot sex, love, and passion on a platter for many days and nights—
only you and I mattered.

The love kept coming like a current to a waterfall.
Your jets just kept shooting me
with a hot, exotic feeling that brought me to my knees.

I just loved how we tossed each other up like a garden salad.
Everything was in it. Nothing else mattered.

It was done from the front door, the side door, the back door,
and even sneaking in from the window.
My favorite was the bareback ride,
because you rode me and tamed me like an untamed bull.
But, like a true professor, I played possum.
Then I gave it to you like thunder and lightening and I made it rain.

You were so blown away by that simultaneous climax
because I kept it coming and coming.
Your mouth opened so peacefully with pleasurable moans of
astonishment.

The love and stimulation were truly there.
The good conversation and mental intellect were strong as well.
Like two old friends—companions and loved ones—we shared.
As God as my witness, I thought you were truly The One.
But, somewhere, somehow, something went wrong.
No more phone calls or letters between the two of us.
My heart spoke to me like a Keep Out sign: *Beware!*

Today, I'm still lost and dismayed.
I'll always keep our special time together in my heart and mind forever.
I loved you then, yesterday, as well as today and tomorrow.
An old friend from around the way.

I will never forget you. I will always remember
the ten days and nights that we shared.

With love always,
An Old Friend

The Blues

It's three o'clock in the morning and my hormones are jumping
sky-high.
What's a man to do?
I don't have a woman, a loved one, or a honey to do.

My Johnson is harder than fifty-ton concrete.
So I get my ass up and take a cold shower, hoping that it will help me.
Now it's just staring me in the face.

I hate nights like these, tossing and turning,
wishing that I had a woman right here, right now, screaming,
"Please, baby! Baby, please! Give me some more!
Do me, Daddy, from the back door!"

I hate this transition-period between girls.
This shit is for the birds.

I need someone day-in and day-out who will love me and satisfy me.
Someone to love me like a real Daddy should be loved.

So, I drop to my knees and pray to God the Almighty,
"Lord! Lord! Lord! Please hear me on this eve.
I pray for that compatible someone
to share my thoughts and heart with.
I want someone who I can cry and laugh with.
I want someone who I can take a stroll with in the park,
holding hands,
hugging and kissing.
I want someone to be with forever.
With this ring, with God as our witness, we would wed.
Is that too much to ask for?
Why do I feel as if I can't find a woman who's down for me and got
my back?"

"Lord, someday soon, bless me with that special someone,
the one for me.
Put an end to these hard-on blues."

Amen!

The Chosen One

The last time I saw you was the first time I met you.
I was truly impressed with what I saw.
(My mind has been fixed upon you ever since.)
I asked myself, "I wonder if she's thinking of me, too?"
Your pretty white smile, your long hair, and your seductive brown eyes
sent chills up and down my spine.
When we made eye contact, I made a promise to myself
that there would be many more moments to come like this one.

What I want most of all is to hold you
in the protective clutch of my arms.
I want to feel your heart beating next to mine.
I want to look deep inside your pretty brown eyes
until I make a connection with your soul.
I want to see inside your mind.
I want to feel what you feel.
I want to see what you see.
I want to hear what you hear.

I want …
I want you to be mine.
I want you to be my lady.
I want you to be my wife.
But first, I want you to be my friend.
I want to have a friendship.
I want to have companionship.
I want to have love and passion.
I want to have trust and honesty.
I want you.
I want you to complete me.

It's written all over your face that something, someone
is missing in your life.
Love!
He is I and I am he, your receiver and giver of love.
This here is meant to be.

I want to put that pep back into your step
and bring joy to your life.
My search has come to an end.
The life that I've known as a single man, a bachelor, has come to an end.
It's all about you.
You're the one.
You're the chosen one.

The Cycle of Love

Our love and passion toward one another are real.
Opposites truly attract one another.
Like moths to a hot flame on a fire.
Like thug life to corporate America.
It's really real.

Our relationship is special
with that extra added flavor of love and happiness, gifted from up above,
heaven-sent.

Together we are stronger and tighter than a lock-washer to a bolt.

Our charisma, our outgoing personalities, and our positive mental
attitudes fuel our friendship
and companionship.
We maintain like the energizer bunny.
Our togetherness will keep on going and going
until our last days on this earth.

May we be blessed with the ability
to fertilize eggs and plant the seeds of offspring.
To be a real man and a woman is not just being able to make a child,
but to raise a child
with dignity, morals, values, respect,
and knowledge of self, culture, and heritage.

Hopefully, this world will be a better place to live in
before he or she is born.
If not, we'll provide our young with the tools they'll need
to conquer the world.

Until then, may we live life to the fullest, like real kings and queens.
We are royalty, you and I.
Remember this always.
I love you.

The One

As I was walking in the park, I saw you standing there.
All that I wanted to do was get your name.
You were the most beautiful woman that I'd ever seen.
I needed to know your name.

I finally worked up enough nerve to come over and ask you the same.
Your facial features, your body's curves,
and the sweet softness of your voice and skin blew me away.

I knew it was written all over my face: *love at first sight*.
Baby, I'd never felt that way before.
It felt like I had known you for years.
I felt a tear or two as they rolled down my face;
I rejoiced because I knew you were heaven-sent.

I prayed to God each and every day that He would send me someone,
my soul mate.
He answered my prayers.

As we dated for a few months and a year, we truly clicked you and I.
The relationship was truly meant to be.
On one spring-filled summer day,
I dropped to one knee because I had something to say:
"Baby, my goal is to rule the world.
The world will truly be mine.
I can't rule this world without someone special by my side.
God has truly brought us together.
I want us to stay together forever, for life and until the end of eternity,
if that can be.
I'll be your king and with this ring, you my queen.
I'll give to you and provide you with everything.
Our love is genuine and true.
It's heaven-sent and I love you.
You'll have diamonds and pearls, a house in the hills,
and luxury cars, too.
But most of all you'll have my heart, my trust, and my loyalty.
I'll die for you, if that's what you want me to do.
Life is truly precious.
It's full of many ups and downs, good and bad times,
happy and sad times.

Baby, I'm down for you.
I'll do what I must do to keep our flame of friendship,
love, companionship, and passion alive.
Please accept this marriage proposal with this ring
and make me the happiest man alive!"

You're the one!

The Right One

As I sat there all alone with the fireplace ablaze,
sipping on a little wine, listening to a few CDs, putting my mind at ease
with the jazzy tunes
I couldn't help but think of you.

As the flames glowed bright yellow, red, and orange,
I pictured your pretty eyes, your glorious smile,
your luscious lips, and your sophisticated look.
Oh, how I wish I could see you to touch you and feel you.
I want to get to know you.

It's all about the mental before we even think about the physical.
Stimulate my mind with your intellectual
and I'll take you on a ride that you'll remember until the end of time.
Baby, I'm a man and my mission is to please you.
My purpose is to touch your heart, your mind, your body, and your soul.
I want to be the next best thing to God when it comes to you.
So baby, if you want a man to stimulate your mind
and treat you like a lady,
I'm the one.
Do what you must do, because I'm the right one for someone.

The question is:
"Am I the right one for you?"

The World Is Mine!

If I ruled the world, I would make you my queen.
I would truly love you unconditionally.
I would give you everything—gold, jewelry, and money.
But what I would give you most of all
are my love, my heart, my trust and honesty.

Life would be so great if I could have everything.
But it wouldn't mean anything to me
if I didn't have someone special to share it with.

Playing the field gets old when you become more mature and focused.
The field is only interested in what you're driving, what you're wearing,
where you're living, and how much money you're making.
The field is not interested in what really matters
like your emotions, your feelings,
your heart, your intellect.

Money can buy you a little stimulation from a prostitute.
But you must ask yourself if it would be absolute, genuine, or true?

Out of millions of women, there is one that is truly out there for me—
my soul mate who will be heaven-sent.

I'll continue to say my prayers, to pray for the one,
the one for me.
I know that God will deliver her to me
when my life calendar says that its time.

When this occurs, I'll not only rule the world,
but the world will be mine!

Thinking of You

As the clock strikes two o'clock in the morning,
I'm sitting here in my easy chair, sipping on your favorite wine.
A sound startles me.
I thought that it was the sweet laughter of your voice I heard.
"Is it you?" I ask.
I realize that it was only the wind blowing against the window.

As I sit here reminiscing about you, I can see your face clearly.
Your facial features are strong and distinctive.
Your cheekbones express the knowledge and wisdom
that your mother and grandmother passed on to you—
your heritage.

Your lips are full.
They're so soft and sweet, like a ripe peach.
Oh, how I crave them to kiss on, to pucker, and to suck on.
Your lips look so tasty that I just want to lick them.

Your deep, seductive brown eyes say it all.
They tell me your life story when I look deep inside them.
Your eyes tell me about your ups and downs, your joy and pain.
Your eyes tell me that you're lonely and that you need love in your life.
Your eyes tell me that you need love, not only to give, but to receive.

Look no further!
I'm your receiver and your giver of love.

Why am I thinking of you?
I guess because I want to get to know you for you.
I want to touch your heart and your soul
with the warmth and joy of happiness,
as if you were holding the sun in your hands.

I want to be your lover and your man.
But first, I want to be your friend.

So, what's it going to be?
Where do we go from here?

Baby, take your time, because no matter what you decide,
I'll always be thinking of you.

Unconditional Love

There's more to being in love than just making love.

A man and a woman must have trust and honesty,
friendship and companionship.

They must know how to do those little things that count the most
like hugging, kissing, and taking walks and picnics in the park.
They must appreciate and cherish
those special and quiet moments spent together.

Listening to one another's opinions and problems
and coming up with a unified solution.
Communication!

Being the other's strength when they are weak.
Lifting the other up when they are down and out and full of despair.
Surprising the other with a gift or two
to show how much they truly love and care.

But, before all of that,
both individuals involved must have a strong foundation spiritually.
Then and only then
will any and all things come to pass mentally, physically, socially,
and financially.

Put God first in your relationship
and you'll have unconditional love that's built to last.

Wake Up!

It hurts me that you're with him.
Jealousy?
Envy?
No, I'm too much of a real man for that.

It hurts me because I know that he doesn't love you like I love you.
It hurts me because he doesn't care about you like I care about you.

The bottom line is that I love and want you.

It's meant to be.
God, the Father, spoke to me.
He said, "This relationship is meant to be because I endorsed it.
Therefore, it shall be."

Now it's only up to you and me to have faith, to believe.
If we're obedient, it shall come to pass.
You and I will be joined as one.

Welcome Home

When you drive off in your car or when you fly away in an airplane
it feels like a piece of my soul leaves me.
I miss you dearly.

I can't wait until you come back to me
so I can hug you and kiss you.
So I can tell you how much I love you and that I missed you.
You are my lady.

May your departure be short and sweet
so you can come back to Big Daddy and make love to me.
I know that as soon as you get home
you'll make up for the fact that you were away from me.
You always do because you are my lady.

I love it when you whisper to me,
"I'll make it up to you. Don't worry, your Boo knows what to do
to please and satisfy you. Big Poppa, you're my Daddy and I'm your lady."

When you come home, we'll take a stroll in the park, holding hands,
laughing and giggling and showing love to one another.

We'll have a picnic under a big, shady tree.
We'll feed each other fruit, wine, and cheese.
I'll lay you on your stomach and give you the massage
you so desperately need
due to the hard day of work that you had,
because corporate America stressed you out so bad.

When we get home,
I'll bathe you and wash off all of the grit and grime from your body.
I'll massage you again with hot oil and cold ice
to make your body temperature just right.

I'll kiss you from head to toe.
Then I'll make sweet, beautiful, wonderful, and passionate love to you
as if it were the day before when you had to go.
Before you fall asleep, as I hold you in the protective clutch of my arms,
I'll whisper to you ever so gently,
"Baby, welcome home. I love you."

Lights out!

What Is Love?

It's been a long time since I've been in love.

It's been so long that it feels like I've forgotten how, but I know it's just like riding a bike, you'll never forget.

Can I have a kiss?

Can I have a hug?

Can I touch you, caress you, and massage you?

Love is a game that you don't play to win, but to survive.

Jelly, jelly roll!

I be strokin'!

I like to do it slow, not too fast; make it last, get and hit every spot as I

Shoop! Shoop!

It's because of you that my broken heart can mend.

It's because of you that I can love again.

It's because of you, my Eve.

As I kneel down on bended knees, I thank God for thee.

Please be mine!

Please be mine until the end of time.

Eternity.

You complete me.

When My Eyes Cry

When my eyes cry, they're full of tears.

When my eyes cry, I pray for a loved one to be near.

When my eyes cry, I pray to God to take away the pain.

When my eyes cry, I pray for joy and happiness to remain.

When my eyes cry, I pray to God that I'll no longer weep.

When my eyes cry, I'm still a man—your protector and your friend.

When your eyes cry, I'll wipe away your tears.

When your eyes cry,
I'll show you emotions, love, and sensitivity the old-fashioned way,
with hugs and kisses for a true queen.

I love you!

Here, let me wipe your tears away
while I hold you in the protective clutch of my love-filled arms
while your eyes cry.

Will You?

When I think of you,
all that I can see are our hearts, our minds, our spirits, our souls,
our fingers and toes locked and entwined.
The thought has crossed my mind from time to time:
What if you went away?
What if you weren't mine?
The thought of this held me fixed in time.
I felt my heart stop beating.
I couldn't breathe.
It felt like there was no oxygen in the air.
So I made my mind up.
I knew what I had to do.
I needed and wanted you by my side.
You!
You here, at this hour; this minute, this second fixed in time.
I looked deep inside your pretty brown eyes.
I held your left hand inside of mine.
I knelt down on bended knees.
And you began to cry.
Baby, all of my life I walked this earth in search of you.
When I saw you, God spoke to me and said you were The One.
You.
I had to work hard to build our friendship, our trust and honesty, too.
Baby the work that I put in,
there will be no cheatin', no creepin', no runnin' around on you.
You're my best friend—my lover and my companion.
You push me to strive to be the best that I can be.
Excellence is all that you want for me.
Baby, you increase me.
You're my Yin and I'm your Yang.
I always want you in my life.
Only God knows how much I truly appreciate, love, respect, cherish,
and adore you.
Baby, it's all about you.
I love you.
I need you.
I want you.

I'm a king who truly needs a queen.
I've chosen you.
With you by my side, there's no limit to what *we* can do.
Your wish is my command.
Here, right now, I'm offering you the world.
A lifelong friendship, a companionship, and a partnership.
You and I will make we.
What's it gonna be?
I want you to complete me.
Will you be my wife?

You

Close your eyes for a minute or two.
Let me take your mind somewhere, anywhere.
Let me prepare your mind for a mission to please me.
Let me stimulate your mind, your body, and your soul.

He can't love you like I love you.
He can't stimulate your mind with the food of intellectual dialect.
He can't stimulate your body and soul, making you shiver and quiver.
He doesn't realize that he has to stimulate the mental
before there can be any physical.

I want you to increase me.
I want to increase you.
I want to be in balance with you—*equilibrium*.
I don't mind one or the other being ahead, a step or two before the other.
It's all about loving you.
It's about lending a helping hand and reaching back for the other.

This is about wanting, loving, craving, and being with you.
It's all about you.

Your Wedding Day

Today is the day that you'll become one.

Today is the day, with these rings and with blessings from up above, that you'll be joined in matrimony as one.

Today is the day that you'll walk down the aisle, hand in hand as husband and wife.

Let her be your Yin and he your Yang.
Let her be your left hand and let him be your right.
Together, forever, until death do you part.
Is that all right?

Marriage: Be in it to win.
It'll be hard because nothing in life is easy.
Let your friendship, companionship, love, and common sense—
with the strength and guidance from up above,
from our Lord and Savior Jesus Christ—
guide you into this new life as husband and wife.

Make me an uncle in the years to come
so I can spoil them like all of the rest.

It's from me to you that I wish you much love, happiness, and success.
It's from me to you that I wish you the best.

On this day, with brotherly love,
may God bless you and keep both of you together as one!

Part II
The Mind

A Good Night's Sleep

As the clock strikes 10 P.M.
on this summer night of daylight saving time
the sun falls low to a bright yellow-orange glow.

The cool summer breeze
gently rocks the leaves on the trees.
The crickets are singing.
The leaves are rocking.
The waves are crashing on the rocks below.
What peaceful music this is to the ears.
Therapeutic it truly is!
Easy like a Sunday morning.

My mind, my body, and my soul are so relaxed,
at ease.

Beauty is only skin deep,
but weather like this can bring you to your knees.

Please don't ever end this peace, this joy.

Continue to play as I lie here until my eyes grow heavy
from the sand that will put me fast asleep.

Cock-a-doodle-doo! It's 6 o'clock in the morning!
Time to get to work, to earn another buck.

Hopefully 10 o'clock tonight
will be just as peaceful as last night.

Off to work I go!

A Small-Town Girl

Dream on. Dream on small-town girl. Dream on.
Your mama and grandma always said,
"Set your standards and expectations high.
In the end, you'll be at the top where you want to be—
amongst the moon and stars."

Dream on. Dream on small-town girl. Dream on.
You can be and do anything if you say your prayers
and live your life like you want to be treated—
with love, respect, trust, and honesty—
how everyone should feel they should be treated.

You already wear the crown of the Queen of all Nubian Princes
and the wife of the Nubian King.

Your color is dark and lovely.
Your heritage and culture have been running things
since the beginning of time.
If it weren't for Eve, would there be an Adam?

Dream on. Dream on small-town girl. Dream on.
A woman is the true ruler and creator of all things.
What blesses a man more in life than manhood itself?
What blesses a man more than manhood is
a friendship, a companionship,
and the oneness with a woman and the Lord.

A man is dead, lost, and crazed without his queen. …
His right hand, his friend, his doctor, his lover,
his Yin and his means of existence.
A queen!
His queen!

Small-town girl, dream on. Dream on.
Remember, small-town girl,
your aim is for the moon, the stars, infinity.
You can be and do anything
because without you, small-town girl,
man is a mere pound of dust, a remembrance of me,
the Almighty.

From ashes to ashes and dust to dust,
the creator?
A queen!

Dream on. Dream on small-town girl. Dream on.
The time is near for you to take your place
and reign as CEO, president, provider, protector,
lawyer, doctor, and laborer.
A queen!

Dream on. Dream on small-town girl. Dream on.
The time is near for you to say,
"I have overcome. I have beaten the odds.
I'm no longer a small-town girl.
I've arrived from a small-town girl to a woman!
From a princess to a queen!
I'm a woman!
A queen!"

A Vision

Fools who want to be pimp-daddies, thugs, and hustlers:
Use your minds to create and develop the future
through technology and invention.
Use your vocal cords to express your inner feelings verbally
toward hatred and injustice in society today.
Keep yourselves in fighting shape
to keep away the plague of sickness.

Use your fingers to write,
transporting your inner thoughts, expressions, and ideals
from your mind to a pen to a pad
instead of having an itchy trigger finger for a gun.

Use your business sense toward the creation
of urban development in the Black community,
instead of using it to commit genocide against your own people
through the use and sale of drugs and guns.
Our community doesn't have the financial ability
to transport drugs from Central and South America
by means of boats and planes.
But yet our community is the leader
in spending billions of dollars
in retail businesses as consumers on the north side,
instead of collecting these dollars as proprietors on the south side.
Support Black businesses.

It's time for us to take a stance
and be true leaders instead of followers.
We must use our knowledge, talents, economic status,
our "pull" and "hook-ups"
to create our own.

Before we can come to the table as one,
we must be able to check our egotistical attitudes
and "crab-in-the-bucket" mentalities
at the door.
We all must be equal and able to vote yea or nay
and leave it at that
without any bickering, back talk, two-face, or stabbing in the back.

Until then, we'll continue to be separate and divided,
instead of being together and united.

Open your eyes to the real deal.

Be true to yourself,
your culture, your people, and your heritage.
Continue to say your prayers and give thanks for your blessings
to the Lord who'll help you through any and all trials and tribulations
that are placed before you.

Remember that He doesn't put you through anything
that you can't handle or bear.
Continue to strive and excel, stand strong and tall,
and keep the faith.

Eta Facta Esta Lux! Let there be light!

Discouraged

I've been away for a little while.
It seems as though I'm losing my mind.
I've been through so much madness
that I just want peace of mind.

From time to time I shed a tear or two.
All that I've ever wanted was to be happy,
to love somebody, to be loved, to have a family, to raise a family.

Some people tell me that I'm special.
They tell me that I can always spark a smile
or touch a warm spot within somebody's, anybody's heart.

If I'm so special, why can't I find a woman to love me for me?

Life is precious.
It's truly a blessing, but it's hard, too.
Sometimes I feel like I'm losing my mind.
Damn! I don't know what to do.

I'm just a man trying to do right.
What's right?
I am what I am, a man who accepts the challenge.
I'm a man who accepts responsibility.

As I walk through this valley that shadows me with death,
I fear no evil.
I walk with God.
He's neither before nor behind me; He walks with me.

I'll overcome!
I'll prevail!
I'll succeed!

I'll persevere!

Dysfunctional Family

My siblings are all about themselves.
You know, the "I" syndrome:
Me! Me! Me!

You would think that with eight siblings
I would have been taught how to dance, play ball, rap to girls, fight,
and cook;
but none of my siblings taught me these things.

Oh, God!
Oh, heavenly Father!
I pray to you on this night:
Bless me with my soul mate,
so I can create a family that is great.
Bless me with a child or two
to spoil, to love, to praise, and to scold.

Bless me with my own family
to correct the ills and wrongs that I grew up with.
Grant me, oh Lord, this one wish:
take away the hurt and pain, the emptiness.

I need this blessing, oh Lord,
to relieve me of this great internal burden and pain.

Bless me, oh Lord, with righteousness
to lead me into a passage of peace,
to wipe away my many tears of pain and shame.

My young eardrums rang constantly
listening to *bitch*, *bastard*, and *motherfucker*—
the disrespect of a king and queen toward one another.

Lord, bless me with my soul mate
to take away the "I" and "me" and make it "we,"
because together, forever with me it will be peace, love, and harmony.

Oh Lord, grant me, your most humble servant,
this gift of family, love, and nobility. End this internal pain.

Oh God, my Father in heaven!
Hear me!
Deliver me!

Amen!

Hail the Queen

Your eyes are of a lighter shade of brown.
Yet they're lovely.
They bring out the fullness of your lips.
They highlight your facial features,
making your eyes illuminate and glow.

Your smile can brighten up any gloomy day.
Such as today.

As your pupils dilate, they reassure me
that your honesty and purpose are fueled
by the warm peace dwelling deep inside your soul.

It matters not what you wear,
for the fabric of your clothes will cling to your body
showcasing all of your God-given asset curves.

I thank God for His creation of the beautiful human creature
known as you.

As you wear the crown of Queen,
which you've truly earned and deserve,
remember in those times of despair, sorrow, confusion, and doubt:
you can and will rule the world.

Why?
Because the world and everything that's in it is already yours.
Go out there and claim it as your own,
as a real queen would.

Soon, very soon, all of the nonbelievers will bow down
and Hail the Queen,
for you will have removed any and all doubt of what you can do:
all things.

Hail the Queen!

Help Me Cope

Good-bye yesterday, hello today, where is tomorrow?

What can you do to take my mind off of this madness filling me up until my kettle whistle blows?

Release me!

Put me at ease!

Lord, help me!

Bless me with a forgiving heart.

Bless me with peace.

Give me balance, equilibrium, and stability.

Help me put in a little hard work, to make progress, to move forward, to achieve.

Can I …

Can I have a hug?

Can I have something to put my mind, my body, and my soul at ease?

Can I have …

Can I have a massage?

I need a drink.

Shhh!

Can you hear it?

It's peace!

I'm a Man!

I'm a man because I can stand steadfast.

Because I can admit my wrongs, my faults.

I'm a man,
not because I can make a child,
but due to the fact that I can raise a child.

I'm a man because I believe in morals and values.

I'm a man because my father was a man,
like his father, and like his father, and like his father, and his …

I'm a man because I don't look down on my brothers and sisters
when they're in need. Instead,
I lend them a helping hand
because it's my creed.

I'm a man because I neither believe in nor live by jealousy or envy.

Because I'm at peace with myself and with God.

Because I'm a strong, intelligent, and spiritual Black Man.

I'm not only a man, but I'm also a King, a Nubian Prince.

Therefore, I am!

A man!

Inspiration

In life, we as a people have encountered many trials and tribulations
where the obstacles were very worrisome.

Through these encounters,
we held our heads high and fought to overcome, to prevail,
to beat the odds.

With faith in God, heart, and mind everything shall come to pass.

There's no need to worry with despair.
There's no mountain that's high enough.
There's no valley that's low enough.
We can overcome and conquer them all.

Every night and day,
life will go on and something beautiful will happen
to encourage us to move on—*inspiration*.

Despite all, the Lord will make a way—
through our prayers, faith, belief, and trust in Him.

All things shall come to pass for us to overcome and conquer.

See it through to the finish without despair.

Keep the faith.

Is It You?

I think it's about time that I met someone
so that we can share a friendship.
A friendship where we can have a dual intellect
that's right there like mental telepathy.
A friendship where we'll know what the other is thinking
before it's said or thought.
This type of friendship will truly be heaven-sent.

We will be able to talk about anything in the world,
from current events and politics
to the animals on the Discovery channel.

I want to get deep with a mate, a friend
in a way that will lead to a *serious* friendship,
a relationship, a companionship, and a commitment.
In a way that will lead to matrimony.

Over the years, a person should grow and become more focused
to the extent that they become tired of the bullshit.
A man or a woman should want to take part in matrimony
not just because their friends and associates have jumped the broom
and they want to follow them.
Wrong!
Stop!

A man or a woman should indulge in matrimony
because it's *meant* to be;
because their life calendar that's kept by God the Father
says that it's time to settle down and become one in spirit.

Life is truly a precious thing. You try to win, survive, and prevail.
In order to do any of these things, you must take risks.

Right about now, I'm ready to take a risk on someone
who's willing, able, and down for me.
I want someone who's ready
for the ups and downs, the joy and pain, the love and adventure
of a voyage that will last until the end of time—eternity.

Is that someone you?

Just a Guy

Jennifer is her name.
She's pure and white as snow.
She's infatuated with a Mandingo she works with
who she really wants to get to know.

Why do you find him so intriguing?
He's so mysterious isn't he?
Please tell us why.
We really want to know.

He's just an everyday guy who's quiet, nice, and sweet.
He's very focused, serious, and sensitive
when he needs to be.

Why do you want to get to know him
and all of these things about him?
Are you not bonded by marriage and a wedding ring? Well, aren't you?

There's not much that he can do for you,
but be a colleague, a comrade, or just a friend.
He's the type of guy who would go to bat for you.
He'd die for you if you were true.
He's a true friend.

All that he wants out of life is a fair game.
He only wants fair play,
to be judged by his character, his performance, and his work ethic.
He does *not* want to be judged by what list he's on,
who he might or might not be liked by.
Can you relate to that?
Can you?

There it is.
This Mandingo is just an everyday guy
who likes to laugh, joke, and smile.
He honors and praises God
for every day that he can wake up and see another day.
In essence, he's being himself.

He is I and I am he.
I'm just a guy who likes his coffee with no sugar or cream.
I like my coffee *black!*

Amen!

Pieces of a Dream

Life is merely a dream.
Every step that you take
represents a piece to the puzzle of the dream of life.
Sometimes we can stand tall.
Sometimes we fall.
The key is to fall on your back.
Then, you can see the sky and have something to reach for:
the sun, the moon, and the stars.
If you fall on your face, you'll only see darkness.
You'll be lost and confused.
If you have God in your life and you fall,
you can guarantee that He'll be a light, a beacon
that will lead you back to the path of righteousness.

In life, we all stumble and fall.
The key is not how, when, or where.
The key to maintaining your balance on your walk in life to righteousness
is to have faith and to believe in God the Father.
Then and only then will the steps that you take,
the pieces of your dream, join together to complete your life's journey.

The path of life awaits you.
The choice is yours—light or darkness.
Either way, life will go on.

Step by step.
Inch by inch.
Mile by mile.
Walk on.

The pieces of your dream lie before you.

Your journey continues.

Resignation

In this battle that we call life,
we fight daily wars that are full of trials and tribulations,
positives and negatives, joy and pain, happiness and sadness,
turmoil and peace.

The key to this battle is to put God first;
then any and all things will come to pass.

It matters not whether you torment me mentally or physically,
because I'm a survivor spiritually.

You can take away my house, my car, my money, and my clothes,
but you'll never take away my knowledge, my wisdom, or my dignity—
my spiritual well-being.

Yesterday is the past.
Today is my here and now, the present.
Tomorrow is the future that I yearn for
in my desire to make a difference, a change.

The time has come to shed the old and move toward the new
with new challenges, goals, and a positive mental attitude.
A new environment.

It's a shame that there are those out there
still trying to bring out the worst in you.
But in the end they bring out the best in you.

My purpose in life is to continue to strive for excellence
and to be the best that I can.
I want to be judged by my work ethic,
my performance, and my character.

No matter what others may say or think about you,
there will always be criteria, laws, and rules and regulations
that a professional will need to follow and abide by.

A professional should not be judged
by the contents listed on someone's
material, social, political, familial, or seduction list.

You're now my former employer.
Therefore, I'll leave you with these liabilities to manage.
Here is my resignation.
I bid you adieu.

Responsible

In life, decisions are made and risks are taken.
Two people are drawn together
by destiny, lust, or coincidence.
Over time, things change for the good and bad, the happy and sad.
A separation may occur.

If a relationship doesn't work out,
it's up to the individuals involved to be adults
and handle the situation in a mature manner.

If children are involved in the relationship,
it's not fair to them to try and disrespect, degrade, or discredit the other.
Nor should you try to turn the children against each other.
The children need the love, the support, and the understanding
of both parents,
near or far, to make it through the separation.

Leave the children out of the mother and father drama.
Leave the adult problems to the adults
and let the children be children.
Support them, love them, and cherish them.

Be a man and a woman about the situation, not a child.

Be an adult.

Be responsible.

Roll Call!

One, two!
One, two!
In the place to be!
Why does the world have to be so mean and cruel
to a brother like me?

I'm just a Black man out here trying to do things the right way.
But to everybody else it's the wrong way.
Life has always been three the hard way.
Especially for a Black man there's no easy way.

Why must the White man be like that?
I should get my gat and rat-a-tat-tat.
But violence is not the key.
Knowledge, education, and verbal expression
will always set a brother free!

A three-piece suit and a fake-ass smile.
Skinnin' and grinnin' in the White man's face.
Sellout!
If it were a Black thing, you definitely wouldn't understand.

Brothers!
Brothers!
Brothers!
When will this madness stop?
You're a menace to society.
Stop selling crack and committing genocide.
The children should be our future, not our past!

Women, you're supposed to be our queens,
wives, sisters, and mothers.
Addressed as Ma'am, Miss, and Missus.
Not addressed as bitches, ho's, and sluts.

Brothers, you're supposed to be our kings,
fathers, providers, and protectors.
You're not supposed to be
immature, lazy-assed, freeloading, looking-for-a-handout,
disrespectful, illiterate, dumb-ass, delinquent fools.
All that you want to do is get high and get over.

Get high on life, the Word, knowledge, and education.
Stand strong and tall.
Put your minds and gifts of expression to work
to overcome and to overturn the bills of legislation
that are against Blacks.

Let's cry because we have peace, love, harmony, justice, and unity.

Let's not cry because another brother or sister
has died before their time.

Amen!
Amen!
Uh, huh!
Preach!

Now, will the real Black men and women please stand up!

Snap!

In life, love is sought; love is shared; and two people,
through a physical embrace and with mutual consent,
engage in lovemaking.

You said that we have chemistry, you and I.
I felt that I should've kept it professional,
but I took a chance and let it get personal.

You said that you'd call me and we'd do this and that.
The fact is that you never followed through with any of that.

You never called.
It was always a constant no-show with you.
What's up with that?
What was I supposed to do?

Maturity and responsibility are truly what you lack.
This is an adult world that you've embarked on with me.
Tricks are for kids.
You should've known that,
especially when dealing with a man like me.

You can only have your "cake and ice cream and eat it too"
when you're at a party.
At a party you can play games.
But my life is the real deal.

A friendship has to be built upon respect, trust, and honesty.
Can you understand that?

My purpose was to get to know you for
your mind, your intelligence, your heart, and your soul.
I wanted to get to know you for you.
From there, anything goes.
That wham-bam thank you ma'am shit is old.

So, when you think that you've developed a little more common courtesy,
respect, responsibility, and maturity you can give me a call.
I won't promise you that I'll be available,
that I'll even be willing to take your call,
that I will even want to talk to you at all.

I just want you to know
that you missed out on this one being the best thing that ever
happened to you—
a friend, a best friend, your yang, your lover, and your man.

I only wanted to get to know your mental before the physical,
but you blew it.
And now I'm gone!
I bid you adieu!

The Big "F" Over

Why did you stop calling me?

Am I too deep and intellectual for you?

Are you embarrassed because your man is miles away
and you felt a connection between me and you?
Now your body's calling for me.

Life is truly a bitch.
It's neither fair nor just.
It's based on what you make of it.
Life is just because.

While you're trying to honor and respect a scrub
by being faithful and true,
he's on the other side of the world playing you.

Life is truly a bitch.
It's neither fair nor just.
I've been there before, trying to be faithful, respectful, and honorable.
But I got lonely and horny.
I deserved a little love, passion, and stimulation.

I gave up everything when the shoe was on the other foot.
It was all about cheatin' and creepin'.
You know, they were out meetin', greetin', and freakin'.
In this case, it happened to you.

Damn!
I got fucked over royally.
Soon, it'll be you.

I won't do it again without a true commitment.

A word to the wise,
my first thought was of you.
Watch out now,
the Big "F" Over is coming for you!

The Finish Line

Life is a big race.

You must run faster
than the person in front of you, on the side of you, or behind you.

Your objective is to win the race.

But your only focus should be to finish the race.

In life, the competition is against yourself.

The Passage

Close your eyes and let your mind wander for a minute or two.
What do you see when your eyes are closed?
You see darkness.
You don't see money, status, or color.
Its just your mind and you.

Imagine that life was lived with your eyes closed.
You're blind and you can't see.
All that you can do is speak, touch, smell, and taste.
Life would be so different, but so great.

There would be no prejudice or hate.
We, as a human race,
would be able to judge one another without the sight of color.
Wouldn't that be great?

We would judge one another based upon our inner self—
our intelligence, our thoughts, our personalities,
our charisma, and taste.
There would be no Black, White, Red, or Yellow race!

Tall, dark, and handsome is what a woman looks for in a man.
In essence, a Black man.

Strong-willed, with full features,
with asset curves cut out with a knife.
A beauty that's deep and an attitude that will make you weep.
But supportive and lovable
in a way that only one culture and heritage could create—
a Black woman.

With your eyes closed,
you wish that you could possess all of these physical characteristics
in this thing that we call life.

But through prejudice, ignorance, and hate you rob, steal, and rape.
You tan to be dark, wishing that you had melanin in your skin.
You have surgeries to develop and enlarge
your ass, your breasts, and your lips.
You wish that you were not you, but me—a Nubian.
You mimic our fashions, our slang, and our gestures.
But you hate us.

You took us from our homeland, the motherland,
to bring us here and enslave us in shackles.

Who are you?
Do you really know?
You and your so-called culture are a fake, a fraud.

Feet like bronze and hair like wool.
We've been here since the beginning of time.
You created the "Great Equalizer," the gun,
to compete with the Black man's endowment.

You created the "Bloom Dress"
to compete with the Black woman's assets.

Open your eyes to the destruction you have caused for centuries.
Confess the ills and the wrongs that you have caused other cultures,
known as strife!

Snap!

Open your eyes!

Welcome back to reality as seen through my eyes!

When He Thinks

When he thinks, he thinks of his accomplishments.

When he thinks,
he reflects upon the trials and tribulations that he's overcome.

When he thinks of joy and happiness,
he smiles and thanks God for this passage he has been given.

When he thinks of sadness, sorrow, and pain,
he cries and prays to God for change.

When he thinks of praise and seeing it through,
he thinks of God looking down upon you.

When he thinks, he thinks of a true friend
who's been there through the good and bad, the happy and sad,
the thick and thin.

He must thank God for you.
Whether together or apart, near or far, God has blessed you.

He thanks you for being his friend and for being who you are—*you*.

He is truly a man when he can recognize his real friends.

His knife is not in a position to stab you in the back,
but to cut a path, to pave an easier way.

He thanks God each and every day.

When he thinks, he thinks of where he's been, where he is now,
and where he can go from here.

When he thinks, there's no limit.

When he thinks, he can do anything.

When he thinks …

When Will the Madness Stop?

Life is a game.
We must play the game to survive, not to win.
Why must we play the game to survive?
Because the overseers of the game will change the rules
to accommodate their own expectations and agenda.

God created man and woman
to interact in the passionate and seductive act called *lovemaking*.
They were asked to be fruitful and multiply.
The beauty of lovemaking
is to express the true feelings, emotions, and love
between a man and a woman.
In many cases, this act produces offspring.

God's purpose in creating this intimate act
was not just for the sake of creating a child.
His purpose was also for the man and woman to raise that child together
with love and affection, with morals and values, and with guidance.

These characteristics are lost in the youth of today's society
because the parents of children
are children themselves.
They, the parents,
carry their own life burdens as well as their children's burdens.

Time is neutral, but with an education, with courage and initiative,
people as a whole can change things.
If we as a people continue to forget
about the past, our ancestry, and our foundation
without the ambition to pursue knowledge
so as to create a better self and society for today and tomorrow,
we're doomed!

If we as a people continue to be "crabs in a bucket"
with no progression whatsoever, we will truly regress,
disrespecting all of the millions of Blacks whose blood was shed
in the fight for our rights, our freedom, for justice and equality.
They will have died in vain.

Please! Please! Please!
My people please!
Wake up!

When will this madness stop?

Let's not just "keep hope alive,"
but let's also keep our people, our history, our culture,
and our heritage alive!

Wake up!

Let's make a better today and tomorrow.
You must start with yourself. Today!

Change!

Part III
The Body

Animal Instinct

Oh, mercy! Mercy me!
The melodic beat of those drums
brings out the wild side in me.
It's like being Little Boy Blue as he blows his horn.
My nature rises and is ready to explore.

I'm ready to run free on the open plains,
to search and find and lay all the game.
I like it when I make them drop to their knees.
No, I don't have any shame when it comes to my game.

It can be a sticky situation.
Especially when it's hot and humid.
It's always hot and humid on the open plains.
Only during the night will you feel a cool breeze
that will make you stretch out as you lie next to a warm body;
a body with thick muscles and sharp curves like a coke bottle.
We all know that the freaks come out at night.

It's best to be experienced on the open plains
because the inexperienced will leave behind much game.
Instead of the young bucks taking their time
walking, strolling, or trotting after and having all of the game,
these inexperienced bucks
want to run and chase after and have just one game.

If you hear any howling or growling near or far
during the day or the night across these plains,
have no fear.
It's just me, "Big Game,"
releasing the pent-up hostility that was inside of me.
If the howling or growling that you hear is a little less masculine,
again, have no fear; it's just my game getting tame.
She's just reaching and releasing her climax as we lay.

I'll continue to roam these plains exploring all the game.
When I'm old and gray,
only then will I consider relinquishing my title as "Big Game."
Until then I'll be strolling and trotting all across the plains
and reign as the ruler of the playground known as the open plains.

As We Lay

As we lay here butt naked, our fingers and toes are entwined.
Our souls are one.
We've just interacted in God's most passionate and enchanting gift to man—lovemaking.

You made my toes curl.
I made your eyes roll to the back of your head.
I made your body quiver from that strenuous, passionate climax.
You made me moan and groan
from the release of that hot, passionate liquid
that had built up inside of me.

As we lay there, we took each other to that intimate high
that only two loved ones can share.
Whatever you want me to do, baby, I'm down for you.
I won't get mine before you get yours.
This is a true sign of a man who knows how to please.
Let's do it again and again until the break of dawn.
You give me a feeling that no one else can—of the highest high.

Don't stop!
Get it! Get it!
Oh, yeah!
Right there!
Baby float on as we lay.

Let me get deep down inside of your chambers of passion.
Let me give you a little somethin' somethin' to stay on your mind.
Feel me, as I climb down each chamber of passion,
as I go up and down on you.

May this cure release you from your daily burdens
"Release me, Daddy!" you say.
My reply, "My aim is a mission to please you as we lay."

Feel me as I caress your body from head to toe,
with the softness of my hands and fingers and ... you know.
May your body quiver and shiver
from the wet moisture of this exotic and slithery tongue of mine.

All that you can say is,
"Daddy, can I have a little kiss to keep me satisfied?"

You said to me,
"Daddy, open me up like a butterfly from her cocoon
and go to work.
Do what you got to do.
Oh, Daddy! Right, right there!
You make my body sing when you go down on me.
I like what and how you do what you do."

It's about time that you turn around
and let me handle it from the backside.
Let's get intimate.
"Can you feel it?"
"Do you like it like that?"
"Oh, yea!"
"Right there!"
"I'm just handling it like a real Daddy would."

Come with me.
It's time to play.
Hold on because I'm going to make your body sing
and your mouth scream.
"Yes, Daddy is at home back here!"

Get on top.
Play like you're riding bareback and ride this stallion.
Slowly is the way to go baby.
Don't rush it.
Let it climb deep inside as you gyrate to this passionate groove.
Throw your head back.
Feel me.
Give me some sunshine.
Show me the stars and the moon.

Baby, I will always be the next best thing to God
when comes to you as we lay.

Caress Me

I think it's about time that you let me do my thing.
Let me play.
Let me caress you.
Let me caress you like you know I can caress you.
Let me massage you with the strength in my fingertips
and the softness of my hands.
You know I can do it real good.

Slowly will be the way that I'll caress you from head to toe.
Shhh!
Can you hear it?
Your body's calling me.

It's okay to moan and groan if it relaxes your mind, body, and soul.
Hold onto your peace of mind
and release all of that pent-up tension inside.

Let me kiss you here and munch you there.

The mood is truly right tonight.

Let Victoria's Secrets sleep while I creep.
I'll be gentle as a lamb
as I massage you and caress you
in the darkness of this love-filled night.

Before I rock you to sleep and caress your body ever so gently,
I'll leave you with this:
A love-filled and passionate kiss.

Clap!
Clap!
Lights out!
It's time to caress you.

Fiend

It's midnight.
Or, it could be half-past one.
My mind is not on what time it is.
It's focused on who's doing me.

I'm having fun loving you.
It's neither a chore nor a job.
It's what I want to do.

Your body is warm and the room temperature is just right.
There's even sweat on the windowpane and the mirror.
I can see our gyrating groove in the shadows from the candles
out the corner of my eye,
as I look deep into your seductive brown eyes.
I'm being kissed here and touched there.
Don't stop!
Get it! Get it!

I like the way you do what you do to me.
My emotions are running higher than cloud nine.
It feels good to me.
You made me feel just right tonight.
It's truly your body that has my mind locked in time, hungry for more.
Our love is stronger
than a 100-year-old oak tree that has fallen into a waterfall.
Shower me with your love.

This is purple rain that has fallen down on me.
Shower me with your love.
Drown me with your passion.
Flood my soul with that thing known as love.
I can't get enough!
This love is the sweetest thing that I've ever known.

Do me, baby, and I'll kiss you, my lover.
This is known as the lust blues of the night.
When we're done, I'll be known as the one who did you all night.

Ding!
Round Two.
It's time for breakfast, lunch, dinner, and breakfast.

Fire and Desire

The fireplace is ablaze.
The room is filled with the smell of chestnuts roasting on the open fire.
I'm all cuddled up in your favorite blanket,
sipping on your favorite wine, puffing on a stogy,
thinking of you.

I hope you're safe as you drive home.
My thoughts and prayers are with you.

As you come into the house, the warmth of the fireplace hits you.
I greet you with a big hug and a kiss,
an "I love you and I missed you."

Your hot mango bubble bath is already drawn.
I undress you.
I bathe you.
I massage you.
I feed you.

As we lie in front of the hot fire,
your body caressed and your stomach full,
the feel of love is floating through the room's atmosphere.

You fall asleep in the protective clutch of my arms.
Hours go by and then I wake you
with the sweetest thing that you've ever known:
lovemaking.

As we finish at the break of dawn, you whisper to me ever so gently,
"Baby, I love you. Thank you. I needed that.
But before we do it again …
the fire in the fireplace is out."

Have You Ever?

Have you ever hugged a man
who feels like a soft and cuddly teddy bear?

Have you ever looked deep into a man's seductive brown eyes
and seen the emotions that are a result of his life's burdens?

Have you ever loved a man
who makes your body quiver with the gentle touch of his hands?

Have you ever been seduced
by the wet passion of a moist tongue caressing you from head to toe?

Have you ever been loved so thoroughly
that your eyes rolled to the back of your head and you said,
"Mm! Mm! Good!"?

Have you ever?

Wait until you get a taste of me.

Then you'll say, "Yes, I have!"

In the Rain

Come upstairs to the attic, to the rain room.

The candles are lit and the flames are aglow.

Take your clothes off
so that they can show your asset curves in the shadows.

Can you hear the rain falling on the roof?
Can you hear the melodic beat of the raindrops as they fall?

Come here and let me caress you
before I open the skylight and let the raindrops hit you.

I bet you've never experienced anything like this before.
Hot sex on a platter with cold raindrops making your ass sizzle,
screaming for more.
I'm just serving it baby, as the rain falls.

Get high on the smell of the rain
as our bodies bump and grind and gyrate
to the melodic groove of the pitter-patter
of raindrops falling on the roof.

Let your body temperature rise from my heating rod
as I find out how deep your love is.

Let your skin quiver from the cold raindrops hitting your body,
making it shiver.

Yes, girl, I'm the Daddy of Passion
who knows how to do you just right.
Just keep it coming until the raindrops stop falling on the roof.
Then hold me like a big cuddly teddy bear real tight.
And I'll rock you to sleep
dreaming of the raindrops falling on the roof.

Is It Me You're Looking For?

Is it me you're thinking of
when you hold your pillow tight late at night?

Is it me you're wishing were there
to wipe away your tears when you cry?

Is it me you're wishing would hold your hand
and massage your neck, back, shoulders, feet, and temples?

Can you hear yourself moaning and groaning
from the ecstasy of being in the pleasure zone?

Can you feel it?

Can you taste it?

Can you smell it?

You know you want it—passion!

Don't deny it!

Stop!

Pick up the phone and call me!

If you ask me nicely, I'll be your little secret
and do everything that you want me to do.

Open your eyes so you can see.

Yes, it's me, the one you're looking for.

Let's Get It On!

I figured that you needed a little peace and quiet.

Sit back and listen to the peaceful and seductive
melodic beat of this jazzy tune.
Let your mind take you there,
in a passage to anywhere that you want to go.
In a hot tub full of bubble bath; at the massage parlor;
or in my room, in my bed, making love
until the cops come knockin'.

Girl, don't you know that I'll give you a little somethin' somethin'
that'll stay on your mind until the end of time—eternity?

May your mind, body, and soul be loved.
May your skin be covered with goose pimples.
May your clit quiver from the wet moisture
of the sliver of my snake-like tongue.

Girl, don't you know that I'm the type of guy who'll make you scream
"Lord have mercy. Give me some more!"?

Girl, come over here and take a bite of me.
Let me freak you and do all sort of things to you.

Turn off the lights.
Turn the music up.
Let's get busy.

Now it's time for your man to show you how he's gonna freak you
and make love to you all night long.
Let's get it on!

Seduction

Come on over to my place.
I have the wine, cheese, fruit, and crackers.
I have a bucket of ice, whipped cream, chocolate Hershey's syrup,
and scented body oils to make your body feel just right.

I have the latest CDs
that will make your head bob, your vagina throb, your fingers snap,
and your feet tap to put your mind in motion for a mission to please me.

The fireplace is hot.
The flames are aglow.
The candles are lit to fight away any evil spirits and gloom.
The potpourri is burning to fill the room's atmosphere
like a passionate aphrodisiac.

The doors and windows are locked.
The Brink's system is on in case any cops or robbers come knockin'.

Girl, I have rose petals—red, yellow, pink, and white—
scattered all over my satin sheets
to remind you that my heart is forever filled with love
when it comes to you.

Now it's time to explore all of Victoria's Secrets.

Come here girl, let me feel you, caress you, and see if you're ticklish.
Let me rub you up and down, kiss your ass, and suck your toes
for a little foreplay.
Bend over and grab your ankles.
I'll pump while you bump.

Don't worry, I know exactly what to do when it comes to loving you.
Your body is a temple that I truly respect, but tonight girl,
to hell with all of that.
This is going to be a legal, consenting rape.
Like hot sex on a platter,
where everything goes and nothing else matters.

Are you ready for this?

Let's get it on until the break of dawn.

It's time for me to handle this!

Zoomin'!

Baby, I'm gonna bring it like thunder and lightning in an electrical storm,
to draw out the wild alley cat in you.
Frisky!

I can bring it like a quiet storm, too.
Like the moon, the stars, the wind, and the mountains
on a quiet, peaceful summer's eve.
I'll make you drop to your knees
and ask me to take you on a mission to please,
like a cool breeze.

I can say this or that, but what it all boils down to, girl,
is quality not quantity.
"Can you handle it?"
"Can you please me?"

Oh yes, I can!
I can make it nasty and freaky.
Or I can be passionate and lovable.
Either way, it will be memorable.
It will stay on your mind every second of the day.

When I get in the pleasure zone, I want to be free to roam and play.
I'll take you away on a natural high.

"Why must I be like that?"
It's just the dog in me to do you like that.

I can be like a wild dog in heat.
Or I can be as gentle as a lamb.
Whatever gets you off baby!
I can even be a tease and make you say,
"Please, baby! Baby, please!"

The question is,
Are you ready for this?
Are you ready to knock some boots?
Are you ready to make love?
Are you?
What do you want to do?

I'm going to give you a coke and a smile
because I'm about to let you ride this.
Watch out girl,
a wild animal is loose.

Roof! Roof!

Part IV
The Soul

A Message

Slowly as I turn.
Step by step.
Inch by inch.
Mile by mile.
As I look to my left.
As I look to my right.
Whom shall I fear?

I'm a man who stands alone.
But from time to time I feel lonely.
But I'm never alone.
God the Father is always with me.

Whether my steps are short and sweet
or long in length,
stride for stride, He's with me.
He never misses a beat.
Left, right, left, right, left!
He's with me!

Throughout my walk in life,
I tried to be the best that I could be.
But only God the Father is perfect, you see.
When He came as the Son people cursed Him,
spat on Him, stoned Him, and crucified Him.
They did not believe, you see.
If the Son therefore shall make you free,
you shall be free indeed.

God the Father gave His only begotten Son for you and me.

Oh, Lord!
Oh, Lord!
I thank thee!

Again!
Whom shall I fear?
Only the Almighty.
The King of kings.
The Lord of lords.
God the Father.

From ashes to ashes and dust to dust,
He created you and me.

There will be no more sickness.
There will be no more ignorance and hate.
We won't be judged by our color or race.

Glory!
Glory!
Hallelujah!
Joy cometh in the morning!

We're in our last days.
I look forward to seeing God the Father in His royal white robe
and His gold crown.
He's the true King.

If I'm alive and well, surely I'll see.
If I'm dead and gone,
I'm sure He'll awaken me from my final resting place
by calling my name.
Thank you Jesus!

I look forward to dwelling within the compound
of the pearly white gates,
praising and worshiping Him and His grace.
I'll be like a little child with much energy, enthusiasm,
harmony, and peace in God's land.
Glory be to God!
I look forward to seeing my biological father, my daddy,
my grandma, my sister, my brother, and my uncle.
Father, God, I love you!

I'm a man who's trying to maintain in this thing called life.
Everywhere I go,
everyone I meet and see,
I carry the weight and burden of my own cross.
My purpose is to be the best that I can be
and lend a helping hand to whomever I can.

If we didn't go through trials and tribulations,
obstacles, burdens, and problems—something!—
many of us wouldn't know the Messiah—Jesus Christ!
Lord, thank you!

Father thank you for whence I came, yesterday, the past.
Father, thank you for where I am—
here and now, the present. *Freedom!*

Father, thank you for where I'll be going—
tomorrow, the future, the unknown, a mystery.
Father, I await you!

Brothers and sisters,
I give these words of expression,
this Message to you from me,
driven and guided by a higher power who's all over me.

Glory!
Glory!
Hallelujah!
Thank you Jesus!

Get ready!
Get right!
The Prince of Peace,
Emmanuel,
Jesus Christ, the Son,
The Holy Spirit,
Jehovah,
God the Father is coming for you and me!

Prepare yourself!

Increase the love!

A Prayer

I'm a man who stands alone, but God stands with me.

From time to time I feel lonely, but I'm never alone.

With God's grace and His will,
He's always there when I need a friend
with listening ears and open arms who cares.

God, the Almighty,
will always be there in my time of need and despair.

Oh, Lord!

Oh, Lord!

How sweet He is!

Your blessings, the miracles,
the beautiful gift of life you can steal like a thief—
a grave robber who comes in the middle of the night.

He shows no mercy when He calls your name.

He will take you in the peace of a sleep-filled night.

He will take you in a deadly, tragic, bloody murder.

When your name is called, there is no place to hide from His sight.

The Creator, the Maker of all things, God the wonderful,
God the magnificent, my God,
the Father, the Son, the Holy Spirit!

I thank you for being you and for creating me!

I praise you!

Thanks be to God for His blessings and for all things,
from ashes to ashes and dust to dust!

Amen!

Amen!

Peace!

A Stormy Season

A storm can be as quiet and peaceful as when
someone passes away in his or her sleep at night.
A storm can be as loud as a bomb exploding,
causing destruction.
A storm can be as mild as a drizzling rain.
Or it can be as rough as a thunderstorm
with lightning that can make the sky glow
as if it were an old, flickering light.
These storms can come at any time of year,
in any season: winter, spring, summer, or fall.
These storms can come at any second, minute, or hour.
At day or night they can call.

It matters not how rich or poor, short or tall,
young or old, or if you're male or female;
nothing matters at all.

It's the season to bring burdens upon you.
It's your husband or your wife, your children, the bills,
your house, your car, your job, and your boss.
It's those little things that pick at you,
that irritate you,
that nag at you.

It's a season when nothing seems
as if anything is going right; all is wrong.
As God as your witness, it's times like these
when you must keep the faith and be strong.
You can do all things through Christ, who strengthens you.

These storms are merely seasons of struggles
to cause temporary inconveniences
in this thing that we call life.

Our Father in Heaven doesn't put anything upon you
that you cannot bear, known as strife.
But during this process, the Adversary, the Enemy,
breaks Hell out all about you.
War!
It can be physical, but most of all, spiritual.

He plays for keeps.
He tries to take away your heart,
but his aim is your soul.

You're a child of God.
You're a solider in your Father's army.
Suit up in His protective armor from head to toe:
the helmet of salvation;
the breastplate of righteousness;
the shield of faith;
the sword of the Holy Spirit;
the girdle of truth;
the sandals of peace.

You're prepared for battle, war against the Enemy,
the Legion of *Doom!*

Whatever the mission you feel you cannot carry through,
have no fear because the angels are here.
They've got your back!

This season of stormy weather is merely a test.
Faith and patience will see you through.

Remember to be steadfast and true.
Kneel down on bended knees,
praying to God the Father for faith and patience.
He'll look down upon you with listening ears.

This storm is merely a test,
a struggle that you must go through to build character in you.
If faith doesn't deliver you from it,
it will surely guide you through it.
This too, a stormy season, shall come to pass.

Weather it!
Weather the storm until it passes!
A light awaits you!
Persevere!

A True Friend

A true friend is someone who'll always be there.

If there's a problem,
they'll be there in a matter of minutes, hours, or days.

You can always count on a friend to call you when you need them:

in times of happiness, sadness, praise, sorrow, or despair.

A true friend will always be there to support you
mentally, physically, spiritually, and financially.

A true friend is hard to find.

Friendship is essential to my soul!

God is my friend!

A Queen

Today is the day that the Lord has made.
Let us rejoice and be glad in it.

God the Father created the world, life.
In this thing He created He blessed us with you.

He built you, woman, and He made me, man.
Some would say that you're the next best thing
to God Himself.
Because you, too, can create life within a chamber, the womb,
that holds the egg, the birthstone of life.

You are truly a queen and should be treated, respected,
and cherished as such.

In my eyes, you're on a pedestal, second in command.
First, there is God the Father.
Second, there is God the Son.
Third, there is God the Holy Spirit.
Second, is you.

Hail the Queen!
Hail the Queen!

These words are sincere and true.
They're fueled by the presence of the Kingdom of God
that dwells within me, that I express to you.

Today is the day that I want you to know
how much I love, respect, cherish, and appreciate you.

The significance and the purpose of this day
have not gone unannounced to recognize and honor you.

Thank you for being you.

I love you.

Get Right!

Life is a precious thing.

It feels so good to wake up in the morning
to smell fresh air, to see the sun rise, yes indeed!

Time is neutral.
It waits for no one.
Every second, every minute, every hour of the day
comes and goes quietly.

Each day to us is a thousand years to God.

Someday He'll return and come back our way.

Disaster, destruction, chaos, and false prophets will reign.

It's time that we all "Get right," because soon it will be
Judgment Day!

Our way of life, how we lived and treated one another,
will be critiqued.

If we pass, we will dwell within the compounds
of the pearly white gates.

If we fail, we will dwell within one of Dante's peaks.

Brothers and sisters: Beware!

Here, in this final hour are we.

Wake up!

Wake up!

It's time for change!

Because soon, very soon,
there won't be time to change our ways.

Get right!

Get right!

The end is near!

Happy Birthday!

The sun shines bright and a cool breeze floats through the air,
putting your mind at ease.

You reminisce about the good times, the bad times,
the happy and sad times that you've endured over the years.

As you look up at the powder-blue sky,
you take a deep breath and say,
"Thank you God for this day, this beautiful day.
With your strength flowing through my veins—
the Holy Ghost—
I am able to see it through yet another day.
You've blessed me, many would say.
Oh, Lord, allow me to see many more days like today."

Happy Birthday!

Amen!

I Am!

As I sit back and reminisce about how it was,
I thank God for my mama and my daddy,
who were sent from up above.

Since I came out of the womb, the fruit,
a reward and a heritage from the Lord,
I have borrowed a thing or two:
Their genetic makeup and a few facial features, too.
But let us not forget the air from the umbilical cord—
the lifeline that was supplied
by our Lord and Savior, Jesus Christ, from up above.

He knew before anyone what type of man I would become.
He saw my whole life cycle—
my childhood, my manhood, my career,
my family life, my wife, and my children—
before it came to pass, before anyone could see.

Only God can project your life
as if it were on a film reel run through the pupils of His eyes;
a film that only He can see.

To infinity and beyond!

Father, thank you for being you and for creating me
and for allowing me to be who I am, to be what I've become:
a son of a king and a queen—a prince!
A man!
A child of God; that's me!
A man indeed, who's honored and blessed to say,
"I am a product, a child of God.
And through He who lives within me
I'll always find a way through my faith and belief;
my salvation that strengthens me."

Father,
only you know where my journey will take me from here.
There's no limit to what I can do when you're by my side.

This is the reason why I live!

Therefore, I am!

Knowledge, Purpose, Peace

Knowledge of self gives you a purpose in life.

Once you know your purpose,
you can have peace not only with yourself,
but also with God.

Keep God first in everything that you do in life

and you'll never be second to none.

All things shall come to those who believe in Him.

Lock and Key

Every day and night I kneel down on bended knees.
I ask God, my Father,
for a safe passage through each day.

Many times I pray for peace and happiness.
I pray for Him to remove
any and all doubt, to relieve the pain.

We all pray for things, but if we simply open our eyes
the answers to our questions
are normally staring us right in the face.

Prayer is merely a means of hope.
We all believe that our wishes and dreams
will one day become God's command.

As we learned from our ancestors,
prayer is a means of hope and belief.
In essence, prayer is a means of faith
that will help us see it through any real-life situation.

Hope, faith, belief, and prayer
are the keys to all of life's mysteries.

Remember, neither leave home nor go to sleep without it.
The key to life is prayer.
The door to life will always remain locked
until you believe in the power of prayer.

Have faith.
Have hope.
Believe!

Midday Prayer

Lord, Father, hear me as I pray to you this midday.

As I look across these waters,
as I eat my lunch for strength and nourishment,
I ask that you help me through the rest of this day.

I ask that you give me the strength to help,
to touch someone's life, anybody's life, in some form or fashion,
before the end of this day.

I pray to you God, my Father, my soul to keep,
to protect me from the evil and error
that might be waiting for me down the street.

Life is truly a precious gift.

If it's time for your number to be called,
you will be known as a memory, what was.

I give thanks to you for my life.
And I thank you for blessing me
with these material things that I possess.
I thank you because I know that with a blink of your eye,
a mere thought, or a wave of your hand,
it could all be gone.
Like summer to fall,
day to night,
it would come to pass.

Strengthen and protect me as I prepare to go back into this battle,
this war, this thing known as the world—life!

Amen!

Mother to Child

Come gather around, my little children.
I have something to tell you.
When I was told that you were conceived inside of my womb—
the egg, the birthstone of life—
I felt a tear or two roll down my face in joy
because God blessed me with you.

Other than being a queen, a wife to your father, our king,
God blessed me with the opportunity to give birth to you.
Motherhood is an honor,
a blessing that was bestowed upon me, woman,
by God the Father.

Every female is not a woman.
Every woman is not a mother.
Every male is not a man.
Every man is not a father.
What I'm trying to tell you is that
in this world, life is not perfect.
Only God the Father is perfect, you see.

In life, there will be many trials and tribulations,
problems, burdens, and obstacles
that will come before and around you.

My job is first, to love and protect you.
Second, to teach you right from wrong
with the guidance and teachings from the ultimate textbook:
the Holy Bible.
Third, to instill in you
self-respect, dignity, honor, self-esteem, culture, and heritage.
Fourth, to send you on your way to make me proud of you
throughout my remaining days.

Throughout life, you'll feel and experience strife, but such is life.

My children, you must live and learn from the good and bad,
the happy and the sad.
This is called experience.

Always remember to use discretion,
think before you act, and use your best judgment.

Remember to never be afraid to fail.
To fail is to overcome.
To overcome is to prevail.
To prevail is to succeed.

When you succeed, my dear daughter,
you'll become a woman.
When you succeed, my dear son,
you'll become a man.

Remember this always.
I love you.
God blessed me with you.
God has His hands on you.
Always keep God first in your life
and you'll never be second to none.

My children, you've been prepared to rise!
It's time for you to go out and claim what's truly yours—
the world!
Claim it!
Conquer it!

My Valentine (Spiritual)

In life, our days and nights
are filled with many trials and tribulations.
We'll face many peaks-highs and valleys-lows
that will shadow us with praise, honor, joy, love, happiness,
sadness, and death.

A true friend is one who you know you can call on at any time
to talk to; to laugh with; to cry to;
to borrow a nickel, a dime, or even a dollar or two;
to share your innermost thoughts and feelings with.

It matters not how late we call.
Time is not of the essence.
You being who you are,
you'll always accept our calls
with open arms and listening ears.

A true friend is someone who will tell you
whether you're doing right or wrong.

There's no half-stepping when it comes to you.
Either we come correct or we don't come at all.
But you being who you are,
you're always willing to work with us and accept us as we are.

You're my first love.
You're my Alpha and my Omega, my Beginning and my End!
You're the light of my life!
Everything and everyone are secondary when it comes to you.

Please!
Please!
Please!
Please continue to be the head and light of my life!
This little light of mine!
Let it shine! Let it shine!

My salvation!
My Lord!
My Savior!

My God, the Father!
Jesus Christ, the Son!
The Holy Spirit!
Jehovah!

My Valentine!

Amen!

Oh, How Sweet It Is!

Oh, how sweet it is to breathe a breath of fresh air.

Oh, how sweet it is to win when everyone thought you'd fail.
Yet you prevailed.

Oh, how sweet it is to overcome obstacles,
trials and tribulations, and burdens too.

Oh, how sweet it is to be blessed with life because of God's grace.

Life is truly precious.

Oh, yes it is!

Oh, how sweet it is!

On Bended Knee

Everybody needs someone special in his or her life.
Someone they know they can count on
to see them through the thick and thin.
Everybody needs an ACE,
who'll help him or her overcome any and all things.

As I kneel down on bended knees, Father,
I pray to you and thank thee.
Without you there would be no today or tomorrow.

Your will is my command.
Your gospel is the literature of my knowledge,
my wisdom, and teachings.
Whatever you want me to do, Father,
I'll be a prophet for you.

As I suit up in my armor to take my position
to fight in this spiritual war about me,
full and drunk on your ultimate power, the Holy Spirit,
may the Enemy surrender, bow down
and accept thee as his Savior.

Father, bless me!
Deliver me!
Bring me back to the fold of righteousness
and give me everlasting joy and peace.

Lord, forgive those who have cast stones
and cursed your name in disgrace.
They're merely fools who have chosen to live their eternal lives
in one of the numerous chambers of Hell that Dante paved.

Father, we thank you for your selflessness
because you gave your only begotten Son
to die for our sins.
If the Son therefore shall make you free,
you shall be free indeed.

Lord, Father, hear me.
Hear my cry for joy, harmony, and peace
in this day and age of ignorance and hate.
Instill in us humans, your children,
a belief that we'll truly reap what we've sowed.
Especially on Judgment Day.

Lord, my mission in life is to live according to your Word
and to live life to the fullest with the highest ideals,
as kings and real men do.

Watch over me!
Guide me!
Protect me as I rise from bended knees
and walk out my front door into this thing that you created,
known as the world—life!

Eta Facta Esta Lux! Let there be light!
Amen!

Our Days Are Numbered

We only have a short time left here on earth.

Live your life to the fullest.

Have fun.

Enjoy it.

Treat others like you want to be treated.

What comes around will go around.

Live nobly, as real men and women do.

But always remember to lend a helping hand to those in need;
it should be your creed.

Get right!

Second Time Around (Born Again!)

If this world were mine,
I would live life as though it were my second time.
I would do all the things that I didn't get a chance to do
the first time.
I would do the things that I regret I didn't do,
the things that I wished I had done before.

I would love you with all of my heart,
my mind, my soul, and my strength.
I would shower you with hugs and kisses galore.
I would always tell you how much I love you and miss you,
even though you're always with me.

Life is precious.
Yet life is short.
You could be here today and gone tomorrow.
But don't worry,
I'm going to handle my business this second time around.

You're truly my heart and inspiration.
You make me smile from cheek to cheek
because you're the Son that brightens my day
that's why I praise and worship you each and every day.
You've truly blessed me with a second chance
to honor, praise, worship, and love you.
That's why I pray each and every day.
You've blessed me with a miracle, many would say.
That's why I praise you.

Glory be to God!
God the wonderful!
God the magnificent!
God the Father, the Son, the Holy Spirit!
Father, I love you!

I thank you for saving me from the evil and error
that dwell about me.

Father, continue to guide and protect me
this second time around.
Guide me through the spiritual, social, racial, and economic wars
that are being fought on a daily basis around me.

The battle has yet to be won, but upon your return,
victory shall be claimed.
The war shall be won!

This second time around, I'm prepared for war,
for battle against the Legion of Doom!

With your guidance and the support from the angels,
victory shall be mine.
I won't be second to none this second time around.
Victory shall be mine!

Strong Men Keep Coming On!

Today is the day that the Lord has made.
Let us rejoice and be glad in it.

Throughout life, history,
many men and women came before us to pave the way,
enabling us to have the opportunities that we do today.
Many lives were lost and much blood was shed in their fight
for justice and equality, praying and hoping for a new day.

Father, we ask and pray that through your grace and your will
you allow us to remain steadfast and true.
Allow us to live as real and noble men do.
Allow us to reign as kings as our forefathers did.
Allow us to love, cherish, appreciate, and protect our queens,
our better halves.

Allow the males, who call themselves men,
to accept their responsibilities and to be fathers to their children.
It does not take a man to create a child,
but a man to raise, support, discipline, love, and protect a child
(as my father did).

Father, give us the strength
to continue to be strong, compassionate, and sensitive.
Continue to fill us with the Holy Spirit
from head to toe.
Allow us to continue to praise and worship you.
Allow us to accept the good with the bad, the happy with the sad,
the victories with the defeats in this thing known as life.

Father, continue to strengthen our faith, belief, knowledge,
and understanding of you.
Seek and we shall find!
Remove any and all doubt of what you can do.
All things, that is.

Father, enable us to work hard and play hard.
Allow us to not confuse the two.
All work and no play make us dull men.
All play and no work make us lazy men.
Father, enable us to balance the two.

Father, allow us to be *real men* 365 days a year—
every second, every minute, every hour of the day—
from head to toe.
Instead of us being *sometimes men* (when we're lying between the sheets)
from our waists down to our toes.

Father, allow us to check our egotistical, got-to-have-a-job-title,
HNC, want-to-be-next, too-close-to-the-man
attitude at the door.

When we come into your House it's all about increasing you
by worshiping, working, honoring, tithing, and praising you.

Brothers, check yourselves before you wreck yourselves.
God the Father is watching you!
Brothers, it's time to make the crossover from boys to men.
It's time for battle.

Father, prepare us for another day.
Suit us up in our protective armor
and send us out into this world—life!

Our community needs strong men with a unified agenda.

Father, show us the way!

It's time to make a change.
Start with the man in the mirror.

Eta Facta Esta Lux! Let there be light!

This little light of mine, let it shine!
Let it shine!

Show us the way!

Increase the love!

The End Is Near

In the beginning, God created man, Adam,
in His image and likeness.
And from Adam He built Eve, woman.
God made Abraham the father
of all nations' kings and queens.

Soon, very soon, God the Father, the Creator of all things
from the dust of the ground and the breath from His lungs—
He will be coming back soon.

Are you prepared?
Are you?

God has blessed us with the gift of life.
We must accept it and wear it proudly as if it were a crown.

It's time to get right!
If your heart is not right, you're not right with God.
When man loses God, he has lost his place,
his means of existence,
his purpose and favor with the Lord.

In life, we must go on decreasing
by repenting and rebuking both our sins and the Enemy.
Whereas our Lord and Savior must go on increasing
through our honor and praise of Him.

We possess a spirit of love, power, and discipline
that is fueled by fear.
Through fear, we have wisdom.
Through wisdom, we are humbled.
Through humility, we have understanding.
Through understanding, we have peace.
Through peace, we have strength.
Through strength,
our faith and belief are justified and magnified.
Through our faith and belief, we have salvation.

Look at the man in the mirror.
The reflection that you see is the best indication
of what your sons and daughters will become:
an image and likeness of you.

A good man leaves not only an inheritance for his children,
but also for his children's children.

He who spares his rod hates his son.
But he who loves his son disciplines him promptly.

It's time to stop taking life for granted.
Life is not a game.
Life is a gift.
Life is precious.

If man lives by pride alone,
his days and nights will be filled with strife.
Stormy seasons are destined to come.

If man, a real man,
can possess and live by the six characteristics of manhood:
sincerity, simplicity, conviction, courage, vision, and vulnerability,
all simultaneously,
life as we know it would be in a better state.

My friends, family, and loved ones, the end is near.
It's time to change our ways.

Soon, very soon, it will be Judgment Day.
Start with the man in the mirror.
Get right!
Get right!
The end is near!

You've been challenged.

Your Journey Continues

In life, we're faced with many trials and tribulations
that make us feel as if we cannot bear
the weight of our own cross.

We must make many choices in life.
Some are good.
Some are bad.
This is called experience.

Knowledge and faith
are the key to conquering and overcoming all.

I can take your money.
I can take your house, your car, and your clothes.
But only you can let me take away
your determination and desire to succeed.

To win is to prevail.
To fail is to overcome.
To triumph is to conquer.

Focus, my dear, focus.
Your objective is to succeed.
You've come too far to turn back now.
The activities that you must give up
in order to pursue your dreams
will become someone else's blessing to endure.

Your strength comes from a chamber deep down inside your soul
that's fueled by your ancestry of strong Black men and women,
the Nubian Kings and Queens who came before you.
They're your bridge builders.
They've brought you this far, over a chasm that's wide and deep.

It's time for you to continue your journey through the burning sands—
FOOTPRINTS—
to your destination,
Wherever that may be.
But remember that Jesus Christ, the Son,
is your bridge and your link to God, the Father.

Continue on your path and do not fear the light.
This light of mine, let it shine upon you.
Follow it!
It's not a train, but a beacon of truth.
It'll take you wherever you want to go.
Remain steadfast and true.
The beauty and destination of your journey rely upon you.

Your journey continues.

Step by step!
Walk on!

MAIL ORDER FORM
for the book entitled

Evolution of the Heart, Mind, Body, and Soul

Description		Total
$16.95 ea		
Wholesale orders	Contact publisher	
Colorado residents please add state sales tax of 6.4% ($1.08 per book).		
POSTAGE (BOOK RATE) & HANDLING		
1–10 copies	Add $2.50 per book	
Wholesale orders	Contact publisher	
Other: (Airmail, etc.)		
	TOTAL:	

Airmail Orders: Add $4.50 per book for orders outside of the U.S.A.

For orders from outside North America, add $6.00 per book. Allow 2 to 3 weeks for delivery.

Make checks, money orders, and P.O.'s payable to:

It Is Written Publications of Georgia, L.L.C.
5819 Campbellton Rd., Suite 108, PMB 90, Atlanta, GA 30331
(404) 683-6691, (404) 346-9554 (fax),
Email: itiswrittenpub@aol.com
Credit Card orders: www.atlasbooksdistribution.com; 1-800-247-6553, (419) 281-6883(fax); Email: order@bookmasters.com

Mail books to:

Name:	
Address:	
City:	
State:	ZIP:

Note: For wholesale orders please contact publisher at the above address.